Adventure is for you!
Brenda Blagden

Ayla,
This book was written, illustrated and photographed by the daughter of my friend Aleta and her husband. She & me they spend a hours being creative, dreaming & planning and setting goals every Monday. They have been accomplish many of these dreams and ideas. I thought this book was one of them. I would enjoy you their creativity. The universe is endless and so are your talents, my love,
Baba

For Skyla and Cedar,
for inspiring us to **A**bsorb the power of nature, **B**elieve in ourselves, and **C**limb towards our dreams.

ABCs
of adventure

BRENDA AND MARC BERGREEN

Adventure is for always- anywhere, any day, anyBody.

Beyond the bold blue sky is a butte beckoning backpa**C**kers.

Climbers use cams in canyons above cacti and campfires. Yay! for playgrounds conserveD.

Downhill due East.

Everywhere in the mountains there is exposure, exploration, excitement, and ediFication.

Friendly forests are fun for foraGing!

Grab a getaway with guides where you can grow, grip, grasp, and gasp.

Such gatHerings inspire gratitude.

Heavenly hikes are heartwarming. Heed the hazards of heights.

Incredible places of isolation are idyllic. They ignite imagination. Beware of itchy in**J**ury.

Jagged journeys will have you jumping for joy like a jacKrabbit.

Kitesurfing and kayaking call on knot tying knowledge.

Learn leadership lessons like "Leave No Trace"

Meander on your mountain bike past moonrise and moonglade to mountaiNtop.

Nautical navigations through nature will help you nOtice anomalies.

Outside or oceanside, you can ogle at oddities like octo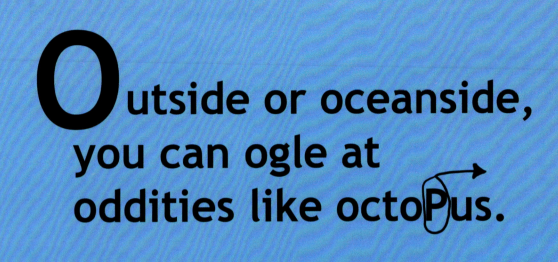pus.

Playtime means paddles and peaks.

Perpetually picturesQue.

Q uiet quests require

you bring your quiveR

Sunshine, sunrises, and sunsets.

Good for the soul, best seen from a summiT.

Uncover an undulating underwater uniVerse.

Vacation in the valley, enjoy the vast vistas, vaporous views.

Wayward wilderness wanderings lead to wildflowers with waxy leaves.

X-factor excellence may lead to

Yellowstone and Yosemite inspire you to… yell!

"Yipee, Yahoo, Yewwwww, YowZa!"

POSTCARD

OM!

to was

(saw)

Zion gives you a zest for the zenith.

Now I know my...
ABCs
next time won't you adventure with me?